MEETING THE BRITISH

MEETING THE BRITISH ⅋ by

PAUL MULDOON ⅋

WAKE FOREST UNIVERSITY PRESS

First American edition published April, 1987.

Designed by Richard Murdoch, set in Bembo type by Greensboro Printing, and printed on Mohawk Superfine by Thomson-Shore, Inc.

ISBN 0-916390-26-8 (paper)

LC Card No. 87-050181

CONTENTS

ONTARIO

I spent last night in the nursery of a house in Pennsylvania. When I put out the light I made my way, barefoot, through the aftermath of Brandywine Creek. The constellations of the northern hemisphere were picked out in luminous paint on the ceiling. I lay under a comforting, phosphorescent Plough, thinking about where the Plough stopped being the Plough and became the Big Dipper. About the astronomer I met in Philadelphia who had found a star with a radio telescope. The star is now named after her, whatever her name happens to be. As all these stars grew dim, it seemed like a good time to rerun my own dream-visions. They had flashed up just as I got into bed on three successive nights in 1972. The first was a close-up of a face, Cox's face, falling. I heard next morning how he had come home drunk and taken a nose-dive down the stairs. Next, my uncle Pat's face, falling in slo-mo like the first, but bloody. It turned out he had slipped off a ladder on a building-site. His forehead needed seven stitches. Lastly, a freeze-frame trickle of water or glycerine on a sheet of smoked glass or perspex. I see it in shaving-mirrors. Dry Martinis. Women's tears. On windshields. As planes take off or land. I remembered how I was meant to fly to Toronto this morning, to visit my younger brother. He used to be a research assistant at the University of Guelph, where he wrote a thesis on nitrogen-fixing in soya beans, or symbiosis, or some such mystery. He now works for the Corn Producers' Association of Ontario.

On my last trip we went to a disco in the Park Plaza, where I helped a girl in a bin-liner dress to find her contact-lens.

– Did you know that Spinoza was a lens-grinder?

– Are you for real?

Joe was somewhere in the background, sniggering, flicking cosmic dandruff from his shoulders.

– A lens, I went on, is really a lentil. A pulse.

Her back was an imponderable, green furrow in the ultra-violet strobe.

– Did *you* know that Yonge Street's the longest street in the world?

– I can't say that I did.

– Well, it starts a thousand miles to the north, and it ends right here.

THE CONEY

Although I have never learned to mow
I suddenly found myself half-way through
last year's pea-sticks
and cauliflower-stalks
in our half-acre of garden.
My father had always left the whetstone
safely wrapped
in his old, tweed cap
and balanced on one particular plank
beside the septic tank.

This past winter he had been too ill
to work. The scythe would dull
so much more quickly in my hands
than his, and was so often honed,
that while the blade
grew less and less a blade
the whetstone had entirely disappeared
and a lop-eared
coney was now curled inside the cap.
He whistled to me through the gap

in his front teeth;
'I was wondering, chief,
if you happen to know the name
of the cauliflowers in your cold-frame
that you still hope to dibble
in this unenviable
bit of ground?'
'They would be *All The Year Round.*'
'I guessed as much'; with that he swaggered
along the diving-board

and jumped. The moment he hit the water
he lost his tattered
bathing-togs
to the swimming-pool's pack of dogs.
'Come in'; this flayed
coney would parade
and pirouette like honey on a spoon:
'Come on in, Paddy Muldoon.'
And although I have never learned to swim
I would willingly have followed him.

MY GRANDFATHER'S WAKE

If the houses in Wyeth's Christina's dream
and Malick's *Days of Heaven*
are triremes, yes,
triremes riding the 'sea of grain',
then each has a little barge
in tow – a freshly-dug grave.

I was trying to remember, Nancy,
how many New England graveyards you own,
all silver birch
and neat, white picket-fences.

If only that you might make room
for a nine-banded armadillo
found wandering in Meath
sometime in the 1860s;
a man-ox, a fish with three gold teeth
described by Giraldus Cambrensis.

Our cow chained in the byre
was a galley-slave from *Ben Hur*
to the old-fashioned child of seven
they had sent in search of a bucket of steam.

GOLD

for Gerard Quinn

You loomed like Merlin
over the class
of 1962,

your soutane-
pocket like the scar
of an appendectomy.

Just a year earlier
old Frost
had swung the lead

while hailing Kennedy –
A golden age
of poetry and power.

Twenty years on you reach
into the breast
of a wind-cheater

for your blue pencil:
'All cancelled;
Nothing gold can stay.'

Not the dead weight
of a grouse
flaunted from an open car.

Not Soutine's
Hare on a Green Shutter.
Not Marilyn.

PROFUMO

My mother had slapped a month-long news embargo
on his very name. The inhalation
of my first, damp
menthol fag behind the Junior Common Room.

The violet-scented Thirteenth Birthday card
to which I would affix a stamp
with the Queen's head upside down, swalk,
and post to Frances Hagan.

The spontaneously-combustible *News of the World*
under my mother's cushion
as she shifted from ham to snobbish ham;

'Haven't I told you, time and time again,
that you and she are chalk
and cheese? Away and read Masefield's *Cargoes.*'

CHINOOK

I was micro-tagging Chinook salmon
on the Qu'Appelle
river.

I surged through the melt-water
in my crocus
waders.

I would give each brash,
cherubic
face its number.

Melt-water? These were sultry
autumn
fish hang-gliding downstream.

Chinook. Their very name
a semantic
quibble.

The autumn, then, of *Solidarity,*
your last in Cracow.
Your father

rising between borsch
and carp,
relinquishing the table to Pompeii.

THE MIST-NET

Though he checked the mist-net
every day for a month

he caught only two tiny birds;
one Pernod-sip,

one tremulous crème-de-menthe;
their tiny sobs

were his mother's dying words:
You mustn't. You mustn't.

THE MARRIAGE OF STRONGBOW AND AOIFE

I might as well be another guest
at the wedding-feast
of Strongbow and Aoife MacMurrough
as watch you, Mary,

try to get to grips
with a spider-crab's
crossbow and cuirass.
A creative pause before the second course

of Ireland's whole ox on a spit;
the invisible waitress
brings us each a Calvados and water-ice.

It's as if someone had slipped
a double-edged knife between my ribs
and hit the spot exactly.

19

BROCK

Small wonder
he's not been sighted all winter;
this old brock's
been to Normandy and back

through the tunnels and trenches
of his subconscious.
His father fell victim
to mustard-gas at the Somme;

one of his sons lost a paw
to a gin-trap at Lisbellaw:
another drills
on the Antrim hills'

still-molten lava
in a moth-eaten Balaclava.
An elaborate
system of foxholes and duckboards

leads to the terminal moraine
of an ex-linen baron's
croquet-lawn
where he's part-time groundsman.

I would find it somewhat *infra-dig*
to dismiss him simply as a pig
or heed Gerald of Wales'
tall tales

of badgers keeping badger-slaves.
For when he shuffles
across the esker
I glimpse my grandfather's whiskers

stained with tobacco-pollen.
When he piddles against a bullaun
I know he carries bovine TB
but what I *see*

is my father in his Sunday suit's
bespoke lime and lignite,
patrolling his now-diminished estate
and taking stock of this and that.

THE WISHBONE

Maureen in England, Joseph in Guelph,
my mother in her grave.

At three o'clock in the afternoon
we watch the Queen's
message to the Commonwealth
with the sound turned off.

He seems to favour *Camelot*
over *To Have And Have Not*.

Yet we agree, my father and myself,
that here is more than enough
for two; a frozen chicken,
spuds, sprouts, *Paxo* sage and onion.

The wishbone like a rowelled spur
on the fibula of Sir — or Sir —.

THE LASS OF AUGHRIM

On a tributary of the Amazon
an Indian boy
steps out of the forest
and strikes up on a flute.

Imagine my delight
when we cut the outboard motor
and I recognise the strains
of *The Lass of Aughrim*.

'He hopes,' Jesus explains,
'to charm
fish from the water

on what was the tibia
of a priest
from a long-abandoned Mission.'

MEETING THE BRITISH

We met the British in the dead of winter.
The sky was lavender

and the snow lavender-blue.
I could hear, far below,

the sound of two streams coming together
(both were frozen over)

and, no less strange,
myself calling out in French

across that forest-
clearing. Neither General Jeffrey Amherst

nor Colonel Henry Bouquet
could stomach our willow-tobacco.

As for the unusual
scent when the Colonel shook out his hand-

kerchief: *C'est la lavande,
une fleur mauve comme le ciel.*

They gave us six fishhooks
and two blankets embroidered with smallpox.

CROSSING THE LINE

A windswept gallery. With its telephones
down and the jiggery-pokery
of *Quantel*
dissolving in the monitors.

Two rival commanders
are dining by candle-
light on medallions of young peccary.

Like synchronized dolphins,
their flunkeys
hand each a napkin
torn from the script of a seven-part series
based on the *Mabinogion*.

Where Pryderi's gifts of hounds and horses
turn out to have been fungus.

BECHBRETHA

At a garden-party in Hillsborough, County Down,
ten or more summers ago
a swarm of bees
rolled all its thingamy
into one ball
and lodged in the fork of a tree.
There was mayhem.
A few of us had the presence of mind
to grab another canapé
and hold on to our glasses of wine.
Mostly, though,
there was a mad dash for Government House.
Once inside, I found myself
smack up against Merlyn Rees
who was hugging his breasts
like a startled nymph.
I'm not sure what possessed me
to suggest he ask Enoch Powell
over from Loughbrickland.
I suppose that when I think of bees
I think of a row of hives
running up the side of an orchard
in Loughbrickland,
and then I think of Enoch Powell.
Believe it or not, Merlyn took me at my word
and dispatched an equerry
to make the call.
I was stifling a chuckle
at the notion of Enoch Agricola
(and half-remembering how those hives are fake)
when the equerry slunk back
and whispered something in Merlyn's ear.
They both left the room.
Now that I had the floor to myself

I launched into a small meditation
on Loughbrickland.
I described the 'brick' in Loughbrickland
as 'a stumbling block'
and referred to Bricriu Poison-Tongue
of *Bricriu's Feast.*
Then I touched on another local king,
Congal the One-Eyed,
who was blinded by a bee-sting.
This led me neatly to the *Bechbretha,*
the Brehon judgements
on every conceivable form
of bee-dispute,
bee-trespass and bee-compensation.
My maiden speech was going swimmingly
and I was getting to my point
when a cheer went up
and everyone crowded to the windows.
A man in hat and veil
(whom I still take to have been Enoch Powell)
had brushed the swarm into a box
and covered it with the Union Jack.
Try as I might to win them back
with the fact that 90 per cent of British bees
were wiped out by disease
between 1909 and 1917
I'd lost them . . .
Merlyn had chosen this moment to reappear
through a secret door
in the book-lined wall
(which raised a nervous laugh
among the Castle Catholics)
and, not to be outdone,
called for order as he reached
into his mulberry cummerbund.
'This,' he said, 'is the very handkerchief
that Melmoth the Wanderer
left at the top of the cliff.'

CHRISTO'S

Two workmen were carrying a sheet of asbestos
down the Main Street of Dingle;
it must have been nailed, at a slight angle,
to the same-sized gap between Brandon

and whichever's the next mountain.
Nine o'clock. We watched the village dogs
take turns to spritz the hotel's refuse-sacks.
I remembered Tralee's unbiodegradable flags

from the time of the hunger-strikes.
We drove all day past mounds of sugar-beet,
hay-stacks, silage-pits, building-sites,
a thatched cottage even –

all of them draped in black polythene
and weighted against the north-east wind
by concrete blocks, old tyres; bags of sand
at a makeshift army post

across the border. By the time we got to Belfast
the whole of Ireland would be under wraps
like, as I said, 'one of your man's landscapes'.
'Your man's? You don't mean Christo's?'

THE EARTHQUAKE

The jacket of her chalk-stripe suit
over a straight-backed chair,

her tie's navy-blue
rope-burn.

A cymbal-hiss
from her eight-year-old's drum-kit?

A goose saying *Boo*
to some great event?

One delicately-tufted lynx's ear,
the fibre-optics

of her hair;
slowly last night comes back to him.

That hacienda's frump
of pampas-grass,

a pair of stucco
eagles guarding its front door.

Her arm goes out to check for rain –
a shoulder-bruise

as from a rifle-butt –
and finds *Radio Eireann*.

Ireland has moved; they haven't.

THE FOX

Such an alarm
as was raised last night
by the geese
on John Mackle's goose-farm.

I got up and opened
the venetian blind.
You lay
three fields away

in Collegelands
graveyard, in ground
so wet you weren't so much
buried there as drowned.

That was a month ago.
I see your face
above its bib
pumped full of formaldehyde.

You seem engrossed,
as if I'd come on you
painfully writing your name
with a carpenter's pencil

on the lid
of a mushroom-box.
You're saying, *Go back to bed.*
It's only yon dog-fox.

THE SOAP-PIG

I must have been dozing in the tub
when the telephone
rang and a small, white grub
crawled along the line
and into my head:
Michael Heffernan was dead.

All I could think of
was his Christmas present
from what must have been 1975.
It squatted there on the wash-stand,
an amber, pig-shaped
bar of soap.

He had breezed into Belfast
in a three-quarter length coney-fur
to take up the post
of Drama Producer
with the still-reputable Beeb,
where I had somehow wangled a job.

Together we learned from Denys
Hawthorne and Allan McClelland
to float, like Saint Gennys,
on our own hands
through airwaves mostly jammed by cub-
reporters and poisoned pups.

He liked to listen at full tilt
to bootleg tapes
of Ian Paisley's assaults
on Papes,
regretful only that they weren't in quad.
His favourite word was *quidditas*.

I could just see the Jesuitical,
kitsch-camp slip-
knot in the tail
of even that bar of soap.
For this was Heffernan
saying, 'You stink to high heaven.'

Which I well knew. Many's an Arts Club
night with Barfield and Mason
ended with me throwing up
at the basin.
Anne-Marie looked on, her unspoken,
'That's to wash, not boke in.'

This, or any, form of self-regard
cut no ice
with Michael, who'd undergone heart-
surgery at least twice
while I knew him. On a trip
once to the Wexford slobs

he and I had shared
a hotel room. When he slipped
off his shirt
there were two unfashionably-broad lap-
els where the surgeons had sawn
through the xylophone

on which he liked to play
Chopin or *Chop-*
sticks until he was blue
in the face; be-bop, doo-wop:
they'd given him a tiny, plastic valve
that would, it seemed, no more dissolve

than the soap-pig I carried
on successive flits
from Marlborough Park (and Anne-Marie)
to the Malone Avenue flat
(*Chez Moy,* it was later dubbed)
to the rented house in Dub (as in *Dub-*

lin) Lane,
until, at last, in Landseer Street
Mary unpeeled its cellophane
and it landed on its feet
among porcelain, glass and heliotrope
pigs from all parts of the globe.

When we went on holiday to France
our house-sitter was troub-
led by an unearthly fragrance
at one particular step
on the landing. It was no pooka,
of course, but the camomile soap-pig

that Mary, in a fit of pique,
would later fling into the back yard.
As I unpicked
the anthracite-shards
from its body, I glimpsed the scrab-
nosed, condemned slab

of our sow that dropped
dead from a chill in 1966,
its uneven litter individually wrapped
in a banana box
with polystyrene and wood-shavings;
this time Mary was leaving,

taking with her the gold
and silver pigs, the ivory.
For Michael Heffernan, the common cold
was an uncommon worry
that might as easily have stopped
him in his tracks. He'd long since escaped

Belfast for London's dog-eat-dog
back-stab
and leap-frog.
More than once he collap-
sed at his desk. But Margaret
would steady him through the Secretariat

towards their favourite restaurant
where, given my natural funk
I think of as restraint,
I might have avoided that Irish drunk
whose slow jibes
Michael parried, but whose quick jab

left him forever at a loss for words.
For how he would delib-
erate on whether two six-foot boards
sealed with ship's
varnish and two tea-chests
(another move) on which all this rests

is a table; or this merely a token
of some ur-chair,
or – being broken –
a chair at all: the mind's a razor
on the body's strop.
And the soap-pig? It's a bar of soap,

now the soap-sliver
in a flowered dish
that I work each morning into a lather
with my father's wobbling-brush,
then reconcile to its pool of glop
on my mother's wash-stand's marble top.

THE TOE-TAG

They became you, that pair of kid gloves
so small
they folded into the halves
of a walnut-shell.

A Rolls-Royce Silver Shadow
idling in the drive,
a Silver Ghost
in the meadow,
their seats upholst-
ered with the hides of stillborn calves.

A jigger of blood on your swish organza.

The intricate, salt-stiff
family motif
in a month-drowned Aranman's *geansaí*
becomes you. Your ecstasy
at having found
among the orangery's body-bags
of peat one pot of sand
and one untimely, indigo-flowering cactus
like a big toe with its tag.

GONE

Since one of our functions is to forget
the smell of an apple-cannery,
talcumed catkins,
the forked

twig astounding itself as a catapult,
the subcutaneous
freckle on a cue-ball,
the story of O. Henry,

what should we make of that couple
we never quite became,
both turning up one lunch-hour

in an auction-room
to bid, unwittingly, against each other
for the set of ten Venetian goblets?

PAUL KLEE: *THEY'RE BITING*

The lake supports some kind of bathysphere,
an Arab dhow

and a fishing-boat
complete with languorous net.

Two caricature anglers
have fallen hook, line and sinker

for the goitred,
spiny fish-caricatures

with which the lake is stocked.
At any moment all this should connect.

When you sent me a postcard of *They're Biting*
there was a plane sky-writing

I LOVE YOU over Hyde Park.
Then I noticed the exclamation-mark

at the painting's heart.
It was as if I'd already been given the word

by a waist-thick conger
mouthing *NO* from the fishmonger's

otherwise-drab window
into which I might glance to check my hair.

SOMETHING ELSE

When your lobster was lifted out of the tank
to be weighed
I thought of woad,
of madders, of fugitive, indigo inks,

of how Nerval
was given to promenade
a lobster on a gossamer thread,
how, when a decent interval

had passed
(son front rouge encor du baiser de la reine)
and his hopes of Adrienne

proved false,
he hanged himself from a lamp-post
with a length of chain, which made me think

of something else, then something else again.

SUSHI

'Why do we waste so much time in arguing?'
We were sitting at the sushi-bar
drinking *Kirin* beer
and watching the Master chef
fastidiously shave
salmon, tuna and yellowtail
while a slightly more volatile
apprentice
fanned the rice,
every grain of which was magnetized
in one direction – east.
Then came translucent strips
of octopus,
squid and conger,
pickled ginger
and pale-green horseradish . . .
'It's as if you've some kind of death-wish.
You won't even talk . . .'
On the sidewalk
a woman in a leotard
with a real leopard
in tow.
For an instant I saw beyond the roe
of sea-urchins,
the erogenous
zones of shad and sea-bream;
I saw, when the steam
cleared, how this apprentice
had scrimshandered a rose's
exquisite petals
not from some precious metal

or wood or stone
('I might just as well be eating alone.')
but the tail-end of a carrot:
how when he submitted this work of art
to the Master –
Is it not the height of arrogance
to propose that God's no more arcane
than the smack of oregano,
orgone,
the inner organs
of beasts and fowls, the mines of Arigna,
the poems of Louis Aragon? –
it might have been alabaster
or jade
the Master so gravely weighed
from hand to hand
with the look of a man unlikely to confound
Duns Scotus, say, with Scotus Eriugena.

7, MIDDAGH STREET

WYSTAN

Quinquereme of Nineveh from distant Ophir;
a blizzard off the Newfoundland coast
had, as we slept, metamorphosed

the *Champlain*'s decks
to a wedding cake,
on whose uppermost tier stood Christopher

and I like a diminutive bride and groom.
A heavy-skirted Liberty would lunge
with her ice-cream
at two small, anxious

boys, and Erika so grimly wave
from the quarantine-launch
she might as truly have been my wife
as, later that day, Barcelona was Franco's.

There was a time when I thought it mattered
what happened in Madrid

or Seville
and, in a sense, I haven't changed
my mind; the forces of Good and Evil
were indeed ranged

against each other, though not unambiguously.
I went there on the off-chance
they'd let me try
my hand at driving an ambulance;

43

there turned out to be some bureau-
cratic hitch.
When I set out for the front on a black burro
it promptly threw me in the ditch.

I lay there for a year, disillusioned, dirty,
until a firing-party

of Chinese soldiers
came by, leading dishevelled ponies.
They arranged a few sedimentary boulders
over the body of a Japanese

spy they'd shot
but weren't inclined to bury,
so that one of his feet stuck out.
When a brindled pariah

began to gnaw
on it, I recognized the markings of the pup
whose abscessed paw
my father had lanced on our limestone doorstep.

Those crucial years he tended
the British wounded

in Egypt, Gallipoli
and France, I learned to play

Isolde to my mother's Tristan.
Are they now tempted to rechristen

their youngest son
who turned his back on Albion

a Quisling?
Would their *chaise-longue*

philosophers have me somehow inflate
myself and float

above their factories and pylons
like a flat-footed barrage-balloon?

For though I would gladly return to Eden
as that ambulance-driver
or air-raid warden
I will never again ford the river
to parley with the mugwumps
and fob them off with monocles and mumps;
I will not go back as *Auden*.

And were Yeats living at this hour
it should be in some ruined tower

not malachited Ballylee
where he paid out to those below

one gilt-edged scroll from his pencil
as though he were part-Rapunzel

and partly Delphic oracle.
As for his crass, rhetorical

posturing, 'Did that play of mine
send out certain men (*certain* men?)

the English shot . . .?'
the answer is 'Certainly not'.

45

If Yeats had saved his pencil-lead
would certain men have stayed in bed?

For history's a twisted root
with art its small, translucent fruit

and never the other way round.
The roots by which we were once bound

are severed here, in any case,
and we are all now dispossessed;

prince, poet, construction worker,
salesman, soda fountain jerker –

all equally isolated.
Each loads flour, sugar and salted

beef into a covered wagon
and strikes out for his Oregon,

each straining for the ghostly axe
of a huge, blond-haired lumberjack.

'If you want me look for me under your boot-soles';
when I visted him in a New Hampshire hospital
where he had almost gone for a Burton
with peritonitis
Louis propped himself up on an ottoman
and read aloud the ode to Whitman
from *Poeta en Nueva York*.
The impossible Eleanor Clark
Had smuggled in a pail of oysters and clams
and a fifth column
of Armagnac.

Carson McCullers extemporised a blues harmonica
on urinous pipkins and pannikins
that would have flummoxed Benjamin Franklin.
I left them, so, to the reign
of the ear of corn
and the journey-work of the grass-leaf
and found my way next morning to Bread Loaf
and the diamond-shaped clearing in the forest
where I learned to play softball with Robert Frost.

For I have leapt with Kierkegaard
out of the realm of Brunel and Arkwright

with its mills, canals and railway-bridges
into this great void
where Chester and I exchanged love-pledges
and vowed

our marriage-vows. As he lay asleep
last night the bronze of his exposed left leg
made me want nothing so much as to weep.
I thought of the terrier, of plague,

of Aschenbach at the Lido.
Here was my historical
Mr W. H., my 'onlie begetter' and fair lady;
for nothing this wide universe I call . . .

GYPSY

Save thou, my rose; in it thou art my all.
In Mother's dream my sister, June,
was dressed in her usual cal-
ico but whistling an unfamiliar tune
when a needlecord

47

dea ex machina
came hoofing it across the boards –
a Texan moo-cow
with a red flannel tongue,
a Madamish leer
and a way with the song
it insinuated into Mother's ear;
'You've only to put me in the act
to be sure of the Orpheum contract.'

She did. We followed that corduroy cow
through Michigan, Kansas,
Idaho.
But the vaudeville audiences
were dwindling. Mack Sennett's
Bathing Beauties
had seen to that. Shakespeare's Sonnets,
Das Kapital, Boethius,
Dainty June and her Newsboy Songsters –
all would succumb to Prohibition,
G-men, gangsters,
bathtub gin.
June went legit. In Minneapolis
I spirit-gummed pink gauze on my nipples.

And suddenly I was waiting in the wings
for the big production-routine
to end. I was wearing a swanky
gaberdine
over my costume of sherbert-green tulle.
I watched two girl-Pawnees
in little else but pony-tails
ride two paint ponies
on a carousel. They loosed mock arrows
into the crowd, then hung
on for dear life when the first five rows

were showered with horse-dung.
I've rarely felt so close to nature
as in Billy Minsky's Burlesque Theatre.

This was Brooklyn, 1931. I was an under-age
sixteen. Abbott and Costello
were sent out front while the stage
was hosed down and the ponies hustled
back to the *Ben Hur* stables.
By the time I came on
the customers were standing on the tables,
snapping like caymans
and booing even the fancy cyclorama
depicting the garden of Eden.
Gradually the clamour
faded as I shed
all but three of my green taffeta fig-leaves
and stood naked as Eve.

'I loved the act. Maybe you'd wanna buy
Sam?' asked Nudina, over a drink.
Nudina danced with a boa
constrictor that lived under the sink
in the women's room. 'He's a dear.'
'So *this* is a speakeasy,'
Mother whispered. We'd ordered beer
and pizza.
'Don't look now,' said Nudina, 'but Waxey's
just come in.' 'Waxey?' 'A friend of mine
from Jersey. Runs applejack
through special pipelines
in the sewers. Never even been subpoenaed.
But let's get back to discussing the serpent.'

I've no time for any of that unladylike stuff.
An off-the-shoulder shoulder-strap,

the removal of one glove –
it's knowing exactly when to stop
that matters,
what to hold back, some sweet disorder . . .
The same goes for the world of letters.
When I met George Davis in Detroit
he managed the Seven Arts
bookstore. I was on the Orpheum circuit.
Never, he says, give all thy heart;
there's more enterprise in walking not quite
naked. Now he has me confined to quarters
while we try to solve *The G-String Murders*.

We were looking over my scrapbook entries
from the *New Yorker,*
Fortune, Town and Country,
when I came on this from the *Daily Worker*:
'Striptease is a capitalistic cancer,
a product of the profit system.'
Perhaps we cannot tell the dancer
from the dance. Though I've grown accustomed
to returning the stare
of a life-size cut-out of Gypsy Rose Lee
from the World's Fair
or the Ziegfeld Follies
I keep that papier-mâché cow's head packed
just in case vaudeville does come back.

BEN

Come back, Peter. Come back, Ben Britten.
The monstrous baritone

of a flushed, ungainly
Cyril Connolly

swaggers across the ocean
from the crow's-nest of *Horizon*

to chide Pimpernell and Parsnip
with deserting Europe's 'sinking ship';

Auden and Isherwood
have no sense of the greater good

but 'an eye on the main chance'.
Harold Nicolson's latest intelligence

has them in league with Goebbels.
And the Dean of St Paul's? –

'Since you left us, the stink is less.'
Then a question in the House.

The Minister, in his reply, takes Wystan
for the tennis-star H. W. Austin

which, given his line in tennis shoes
(though not the soup-stained ties

and refusal ever to change his smalls)
seems just. Perhaps the Dean of St Paul's

himself did time
with Uncle Wizz in an airless room

(a collaboration on *John* Bunyan?)
and has some grounds for his opinion.

In this, as in so many things,
it won't be over till the fat lady sings.

CHESTER

The fat lady sings to Der Rosenkavalier
Die Zeit, die ist ein sonderbar Ding;
in time Octavian will leave her
for Sophie, Sophie

leave Ochs:
Feldmarschalls trade their Marschallins
for those time-honoured trophies –
cunts, or fresh, young cocks.

Among the miscellaneous
Jack Tars
I met last week in a Sands Street bar

I came on one whose uncircumcised dong's
sand-vein was a seam of beryl, abstruse
as this lobster's.

SALVADOR

This lobster's not a lobster but the telephone
that rang for Neville Chamberlain.

It droops from a bare branch
above a plate, on which the remains of lunch

include a snapshot of Hitler
and some boiled beans left over

from *Soft Construction: A Premonition
of Civil War.* When Breton

hauled me before his kangaroo-court
I quoted the Manifesto; we must disregard

moral and aesthetic considerations
for the integrity of our dream-visions.

What if I dreamed of Hitler as a masochist
who raises his fist

only to be beaten?
I might have dreamed of fucking André Breton

he so pooh-poohed my *Enigma of William Tell.*
There I have Lenin kneel

with one massive elongated buttock
and the elongated peak

of his cap supported by two forked sticks.
This time there's a raw beef-steak

on the son's head. My father croons a lullaby.
Is it that to refer, however obliquely,

is to refer? In October, 1934,
I left Barcelona by the back door

with a portfolio of work
for my first one-man show in New York.

A starry night. The howling of dogs.
The Anarchist taxi-driver carried two flags,

Spanish and Catalan. Which side was I on?
Not one, or both, or none.

I who had knelt with Lenin in Breton's court
and sworn allegiance to the proletariat

had seen the chasm
between myself and surrealism

begin as a hair-crack on a tile.
In *Soft Construction* I painted a giant troll

tearing itself apart limb
by outlandish limb.

Among the broken statues of Valladolid
there's one whose foot's still welded

to the granite plinth
from which, like us, it draws its strength.

From that, and from those few boiled beans.
We cannot gormandize upon

the flesh of Cain and Abel
without some melancholic vegetable

bringing us back to earth, to the boudoir
in the abattoir.

Our civil wars, the crumbling of empires,
the starry nights without number

safely under our belts,
have only slightly modified the tilt

of the acanthus leaf,
its spiky puce-and-alabaster an end in itself.

CARSON

In itself, this old, three-storey brownstone
is unremarkable, and yet so vivid was the reverie
in which it appeared to George one night
that when he drove
next morning to Brooklyn Heights
he found it true. I had just left Reeves
and needed a place to stay. As must Wynstan,

dear Wynnie-Pooh, who's given to caution
the rest of us every
time we sit down, be it to jerky
or this afternoon's Thanksgiving dinner, every
blessed time, 'We'll have crawfish, turkey,
salad and savoury,
and no political discussion' –

a form of grace
that would surely have raised an eyebrow
at even the Last Supper,
never mind a household where no time ago
when the Richard Wrights moved in the super
moved out, unwilling, it seemed, to draw and hew
and tend the furnace for fellow Negroes.

Nothing is too much bother
for Eva, our cook, a former Cotton Club chorine
whom Gypsy found, who can so glamourize
pork-belly, grits and greens
I imagine myself back in Columbus,
Georgia, imagine, indeed a paddle-steamer careen
and clarion up the East River

from the Chattahoochee, its cargo of blue dimity,
oil lamps and the things
of childhood washed
overboard; my Christmas stocking
limps from the stern like an oriole's nest:
when an orange in the toe spreads it black wing
the stocking, too, is empty.

The magnolia tree at my window's a bonsai
in the glass globe
I jiggle like a cocktail-
waiter from the Keynote Club,
so that Chester's Kwakiutl
false-face and glib,
Jane and Paul Bowles, the chimpanzee

and its trainer, Gypsy
and hers, are briefly caught up in an eddy
of snow; pennies
from heaven, Wynstan's *odi*
atque amo of seconal and bennies:
then my cloudy
globe unclouds to reveal the tipsy

MacNeice a monarch
lying in state on a Steinway baby grand
between the rotting
carcasses of two pack-mules from *Un Chien Andalou*
while a strait-laced Benjamin Britain
picks out a rondo
in some elusive minor key.

If only I might as readily dismiss
the chord a fire-siren struck
in all of us this afternoon (we chased the engines
two or three blocks
till we tired) or the ingenuous
slow-slow-quick
I felt again for Reeves – the Dismas

on my right side – or Erika Mann's
piercing my left
as we stood in Cranberry Street; flute-music,
panting of hinds, her spindrift
gaze; peacocks, sandalwood, the musky
otto of her cleft:
two girls, I thought, two girls in silk kimonos.

LOUIS

Both beautiful, one a gazebo.
When Hart Crane fell
from the *Orizaba*
it was into the *trou normand* of the well

at Carrickfergus castle.
All very Ovidian,
as the ghostly
Healfdene

once remarked of both sorts of kipper
we were forced to eat
at supper

every night in Reykjavik;
one tasted of toe-nails, one of the thick
skin on the soles of the feet.

He now affects an ulster lined with coypu
and sashays like an albino rabbit
down the same Fifth Avenue
where Avida Dollars
once squired an ocelot
on a solid
gold chain snaffled from Bonwit Teller's.
It seems that Scott Fitzgerald wrote *Ivanhoe*
or the *Rubáiyát*
and Chester Kallman = Agape.

Wystan likes to tell how he lost his faith
in human nature

in a movie-theatre
at 85th

and York, where the neighbourhood Huns
had taken a break from baking buns

to egg
on Hitler to his *Sieg*

im Poland; the heavy bear that went to bed
with Delmore Schwartz was bad

and the rye in Yorkville's *Schwartzbrot*
shot through with ergot.

Since when he's set himself up as a stylite
waiting for hostilities

58

to cease, a Dutch master
intent only on painting an oyster

or lemon
(all those afternoons in the Ashmolean)

or the slur of light in a red goblet
while Montagues and Capulets

run riot, as they did five years ago
in the Short Strand and Sandy Row.

Then my father preached 'Forget the past'
and episcopized

into the wind
and again refused to sign the Covenant;

though the seam of gold a Unitedman strikes
in Wicklow in 1796

which Parnell will later pan and assay
to make a ring for Kitty O'Shea

was well and truly played
out, no bishop could ever quite contemplate

a life merely nasty, British and short.
Delmore was ushered

from that same movie-theatre
with 'Everything you do matters';

the displacement of soap-suds in a basin
may have some repercussion

for a distant ship:
only last night I tried to butt the uneven

pages of a *Belfast Newsletter* from 1937
into some sort of shape . . .

Imagine a great white highway
a quarter of a mile broad
extending the length of Ireland
from the Giant's Causeway
to Mizen Head
and you can grasp the magnitude
of our annual output of linen.

Among the blue flowers of the flax a linnet
sang out 'Lundy'

at the implications of that bleach-
green. 'It was merely a figure of speech.'

'Call it what you like.
The grey skies of an Irish Republic

are as nothing compared to this blue dome.'
He tailed off over the flax-dam

to return with a charm of goldfinches
who assailed me with their 'Not an inch'

and their 'No', and yet again, 'No'.
As they asperged me with kerosene

I recognized the voice of Sir Edward Carson;
'Bid me strike a match and blow.'

In dreams begin responsibilities;
it was on account of just such an allegory
that Lorca
was riddled with bullets

and lay mouth-down
in the fickle shadow of his own blood.
As the drunken soldiers of the *Gypsy Ballads*
started back for town

they heard him calling through the mist,
'When I die leave the balcony shutters open.'
For poetry *can* make things happen –
not only can, but *must* –

and the very painting of that oyster
is in itself a political gesture.

As O'Daly well knows. It was in the olive-grove
where Lorca's buried
that he envisaged *Two Pieces of Bread
Expressing the Idea of Love*

with its miniature duellists and chess-pawn
expressing also his idea of Spain.
(If only he were here
today to make his meaning absolutely clear.)

So that, for me, brandy and smoked
quail and a crumpled baguette
conjure O'Daly, then themselves, then Beckett's
'¡Uptherepublic!',

then Beatrice and Benedick
in the back seat of Eleanor's mother's Pontiac.

After drinking all night in a Sands Street shebeen
where a sailor played a melodeon
made from a merman's spine
I left by the back door of Muldoon's

(it might have been the Rotterdam)
on a Monday morning, falling in with
the thousands of shipyardmen who tramped
towards the front gates of Harland and Wolff.

The one-eyed foreman had strayed out of Homer;
'MacNeice? That's a Fenian name.'
As if to say, 'None of your sort, none of you

will as much as go for a rubber hammer
never mind chalk a rivet, never mind caulk a seam
on the quinquereme of Nineveh.'

NOTES

"7, Middagh Street" takes its name from the Brooklyn-Heights residence of George Davis, fiction editor for *Harper's Bazaar*. In the autumn of 1940, W.H. Auden, Chester Kallman, Gypsy Rose Lee, Benjamin Britten, Peter Pears, Salvador Dali, Carson McCullers, Louis MacNeice, Paul and Jane Bowles, and a trained chimpanzee were among the residents and visitors there.

In his mid-thirties, Paul Muldoon has published four volumes of poetry and a volume of selected poems and edited the *Faber Book of Contemporary Irish Poetry*. Formerly a producer for BBC in Belfast, Muldoon taught a year at Cambridge before departing for New York to teach at Columbia and Princeton.

Mules and Early Poems (1973, 1977; rev. 1985), *Why Brownlee Left* (1980), and *Quoof* (1983) are available from Wake Forest University Press.

The cover illustration *A Group of Cavalry in the Snow* by Ernest Meissonier (1815-91) is used with permission of the National Gallery of Ireland.

ACKNOWLEDGEMENTS

Acknowledgements are due to the editors of *Antaeus, Aquarius, Cambridge Review, The Faber Book of Political Verse, Field, Honest Ulsterman, Irish Press, Irish Times, London Review of Books, Massachusetts Review, New Statesman, North, Observer, Oxford Poetry, Poetry Book Society Supplement* (Winter 1983), *Poetry Ireland Review, Poetry Review, With a Poet's Eye* (Tate Gallery), *Times Literary Supplement*: several of these poems were included in a pamphlet, *The Wishbone* (Gallery Press, 1984).

I am also grateful to Aosdána, the Arts Council of Northern Ireland, and the Judith E. Wilson Fund.